To Rosa Marshall
Be Affirmed!
Peace and Blessings!
Kanisha L. Adkins
10-6-2019

LESS THAN VIRTUOUS
MORE THAN CAPABLE

Affirmations for Everyday Women

*Exploring, Embracing, and Affirming the
Strength of Women Named in the Old Testament*

Kanisha L. Adkins

3E Publishing
Glen Allen

D1319589

All Titles (Paperbacks and eBooks)
Availabe on www.Amazon.com

This book is dedicated to my mother and my father, Carleen and Rufus, my sister Selina, my niece Marquia, and my nephew Michael.

CONTENTS

ACKNOWLEDGMENTS

Angela Henderson and Tracey Prince Ross, thank you for allowing me to use you as a 'focus group'. We've known each other for more than 35 years. In the words of a familiar song, "Thank you for being a friend." Rev. Littycia Clay-Crawley and Rev. Connie Parker, thank you for your feedback. The modifications you suggested added so much to this work. Galaxy Systems Corporations, thank you for another excellent editorial experience and for reminding me to stay in my own voice.

Wyvetra Hill (loctitian and stylist), and Anita Hill-Moses (loctitian, stylist and owner of Braids and Dreds Natural Hair Salon, Inc., Richmond, Virginia), many, many thanks to you for styling my hair for the photo shoot. You never disappoint. Clifton Gunn Photography, thank you for another amazing and fun photo shoot and another awesome photo for my book cover. Syreeta Bailey Stewart, Esquire, thanks again for giving me access to yet another perfect setting for my photo shoot. Selina, Marquia, Michael, Clif and Shara, thank you for weighing in on the cover design. Alana Robinson, thank you so much for your technical expertise and help with the cover and manuscript layout.

And always, To God Be the Glory!

INTRODUCTION

Have you ever heard of the *Proverbs 31 Woman*? You can find a description of her in the Bible – Proverbs 31:10-31. Different biblical versions describe her using different words: competent – noble – excellent. But the most well-known description, *a virtuous woman*, is in the King James Version.

The writer of Proverbs 31 paints a picture of a perfect woman, a virtuous woman. This virtuous woman is a wife, a mother, the supervisor of her house, which includes servants, and a manager of a thriving, profitable business. This virtuous woman is polished and desirable. She is the fantasy, the dream, the goal. But the reality of the Bible is everyday women who often fall short of the goal.

Most of the women in the various books of the Old Testament are frequently portrayed in less than flattering and idealistic terms. They don't supervise households and manage outside businesses. Their jobs are daughter, wife, mother, sister and slave. Their significance is based on their relationships with sons, husbands, fathers, brothers, uncles and masters.

The women are portrayed as insecure, conniving, self-serving, defiant, overlooked, and disposable. They aren't described as having the qualities of the Proverbs 31 *Virtuous Woman*. They are everyday women who are, at times, *messy*. But they are everyday women who are always *marvelous*, in spite of their messiness.

These everyday women are often presented as *less than virtuous*, but they have stories that reveal strengths that are worthy of affirmation and that show they are *more than capable*. And while the Bible writers have often neglected to include their stories and their strengths, in many instances, the writers have shared their names – unlike the Proverbs 31 *Virtuous Woman* who is given great attributes, but who is *nameless*.

This is a book of daily affirmations for women, inspired by women *named* in the Old Testament of the Bible. It isn't simply a *re-telling* of stories that have been handed down through various versions and translations of the Bible. This book is written with the *women* as the main characters of the stories – not just a man's wife or concubine. Not just a man's sister, daughter or mother.

The stories are inspired by verses and passages in the Bible. In those passages where there is no story, but only a name, I've used my *sanctified imagination* and given each woman a story – *her story* – exploring what she might have thought and felt, and what she might have said and done, if the story had been told from her point of view. Not only is each story told from the woman's point of view, each story is told with the purpose of highlighting the woman's strength. Because every woman has a story and every woman has strength.

Strength doesn't grow out of ease. Strength is birthed out of struggle – struggle to get out of messy, dark, painful, chaotic places. And even when the stories show women experiencing, and in some instances causing pain, heart-ache and death, a holistic reading and understanding of the text reveals strengths that are worthy of affirmation.

Read this book as you would read a book of daily devotionals. Read the stories and *explore the strengths of the women* named in the Old Testament. Some of the names will be familiar to you, like Eve, Sarah and Miriam. But there are other names that you may not know like Asenath, Elisheba and Shelomith. These women and many others are named in the Bible. It's time for us to know their names and stories, and to allow them to inspire us.

And even though your specific story may be different from their stories, *embrace their strengths* as your own. Pages are included for you to write *Your Story—Your Strength*. Whatever your problem, your situation, or your predicament, there is redeeming strength in you. Tell your story and *affirm your strength*.

EVE

Inspired by Genesis 3:1-16

*****

The Scripture

To the woman he said, "I will greatly increase your pangs in childbearing; in pain you shall bring forth children, yet your desire shall be for your husband, and he shall rule over you."

Genesis 3:16 (New Revised Standard Version)

*****

Her Story

Eve couldn't believe what was happening. The day had started out so perfectly. In fact, life had seemed perfect. She had only been married a few days to a man who had vowed to protect her and love her. God had blessed them to live in a beautiful garden and was providing them with everything they needed. She *couldn't* imagine life getting any better. And *she never* imagined that it would get worse – but it did.

God had told Eve and her husband, Adam, not to eat from the Tree of Knowledge and, if they did, that they would die. But the serpent told them eating the fruit would make them wise and intelligent. It would make them like God. Eve and Adam thought it would be great to be like God. So, they ate the fruit. But as soon as they ate it, instead of feeling better – which is what Eve assumed she would feel as a result of being wiser, more intelligent and like God – she felt horrible. And so did Adam. *Eve wondered if this feeling was death.*

The day had started out so perfectly. And now Eve was being blamed by her husband for disobeying God. Adam had been right beside her when God gave them instructions not to eat the fruit. She hadn't forced him to do anything he didn't want to do. He had eaten, of his own free will, but here he was blaming her. She couldn't believe that the man who had just days earlier declared his love for her now intended for her to take all of the blame for their *collective* disobedience.

And even worse, Eve felt God put extra blame on her. Sure, Adam and the serpent were punished, but Eve felt her punishment was extreme and excessive. "*In pain – you will bear children.*" That's what God told her. Every time she gave birth, she would experience pain. Giving birth and bringing life into the world – the very thing that should have been a blessing and filled her with joy – would somehow be connected to pain. *Surely, this* had to be what *death* felt like.

It was almost unbearable. It *would* have been unbearable if Eve hadn't decided to focus on *life*. Instead of focusing on *death*, she would focus on *life*. Instead of focusing on *pain,* she would focus on *life*. She would focus on *life* because she was a *life-giver*.

*****

Strength Affirmations

I will make my pain count. Even in pain, I can be productive. I will give life.

*****

Your Story—Your Strength

In what areas of your life have you
or will you affirm these strengths?

_____

_____

_____

_____

_____

_____

_____

_____

_____

_____

_____

_____

_____

_____

_____

_____

_____

_____

_____

_____

_____

_____

ADAH & ZILLAH

Inspired by Genesis 4:13-24

*****

The Scripture

"Lamech took two wives; the name of the one was Adah, and the name of the other Zillah." Genesis 4:19

*****

Her Story

Adah and Zillah knew they would be taken as wives, but they never thought they would be wives to the same man. It was unheard of for a man to take more than one wife. For some reason their parents agreed to give both of them as wives to a man named Lamech. Lamech was a powerful man in the community and he acted as if he deserved to have whatever he wanted. He could be quite intimidating. And he was often in a foul mood. Adah and Zillah often talked about whether Lamech might have intimidated their parents into breaking the tradition of "one man, one wife."

One day, while Adah and Zillah were preparing the evening meal, their sons came home. They greeted their mothers and began to talk about how well the day had gone. Lamech had come in with them but he was in his usual foul mood and said nothing. When the boys went outside to get water, Lamech yelled at the two women. "Listen to me! Both of you! Listen to me! A man wounded me and a boy hit me. I killed them both. If anyone ever tries to hurt me, it'll be ten times worse for that person than it was for anyone who ever tried to hurt my grandfather Cain." Without another word, he turned around and went outside to be with his sons.

Adah and Zillah had no idea what he was talking about. They lived in a small community and hadn't heard about anyone being killed. They wondered whether Lamech was talking about something that happened that day. And if it happened that day, why hadn't their sons mentioned it? Or was he talking about something he had done before he took them to be his wives?

Adah and Zillah were confused by Lamech's outburst. But what confused them more was that he shared this bit of information with them. He never told them things like this. He never said much to them. So why, they wondered, was he telling them this? Did he really kill someone? Or was he trying to intimidate them in the same way that he intimidated most people? His mood had grown worse after Zillah had given birth to a daughter, whom she named Naamah. It was no secret that Lamech preferred sons. They were more valuable to him. Could this have been the reason?

Whatever his reasons were, Adah and Zillah were determined that they wouldn't allow Lamech to intimidate them. He was powerful, but the truth was that he needed them, more than he would ever admit. And whether he had actually killed a man or not, Adah and Zillah refused to live in fear.

*****

Strength Affirmations

I can stand up to bullies and threats. I will not be intimidated by insecure people. I will not live in fear.

*****

Your Story—Your Strength

In what areas of your life have you
or will you affirm these strengths?

_____

_____

_____

_____

_____

_____

_____

_____

_____

_____

_____

_____

_____

_____

_____

_____

_____

_____

_____

_____

_____

ISCAH & MILCAH

Inspired by Genesis 11:27-31

*****

The Scripture

"Abram and Nahor took wives; the name of Abram's wife was Sarai, and the name of Nahor's wife was Milcah. She was the daughter of Haran the father of Milcah and Iscah." Genesis 11:29

*****

Her Story

There were a lot of changes going on in Iscah's life. She had overheard her grandfather, Terah, talking about a place called Canaan. He said life was good for them in Ur, but he thought it could be better in Canaan. So Terah decided that he would move to Canaan and he would take Abram, Iscah's uncle, with him. Abram was married, so his wife Sarai would go, too. Iscah also overheard that her brother Lot would go. He could help them find land and get settled.

The conversations went on for months. They talked about Nahor, Iscah's other uncle. He had planned to go too but then decided to take Milcah, Iscah's sister, as his wife. He and Milcah would stay in Ur until everyone else was settled in Canaan. Plans were being made for everyone, Iscah noticed, except her.

Terah didn't think Iscah would be much help to him in setting up their new home in Canaan. It would be hard work and it might even be dangerous. It was new territory and they didn't know what they'd encounter. And Nahor didn't seem to be excited about Iscah staying in Ur. If she stayed in Ur, he would eventually either have to take her as a wife or have to find a husband for her before leaving for Canaan. But at the present time, she wasn't old enough to have children and couldn't be taken as a wife.

Iscah heard all of the conversations about her. Terah didn't think it would be beneficial to him to take her to Canaan. Nahor didn't think it would be beneficial to him to keep her in Ur. No one asked her whether she wanted to stay or go. She knew that her opinion didn't matter. But she also knew that they couldn't act like she didn't exist. They would have to provide for her because she was part of the family.

*****

Strength Affirmations

My presence validates me.
I am valuable because I exist.

*****

Your Story—Your Strength

In what areas of your life have you
or will you affirm these strengths?

_____

_____

_____

_____

_____

_____

_____

_____

_____

Kanisha L. Adkins

_____

_____

_____

_____

_____

_____

_____

_____

_____

_____

_____

_____

HAGAR

Inspired by Genesis 16

*****

The Scripture

"And he said, "Hagar, slave-girl of Sarai, where have you come from and where are you going?" She said, "I am running away from my mistress Sarai.""
Genesis 16:8

*****

Her Story

Hagar had tried to have sympathy for Sarai. After all, it was no secret what Abram had done to her. When they first came to Egypt to escape the drought and famine in their country, Abram denied that Sarai was his wife because he feared the Egyptian king would kill him and take Sarai. He said Sarai was his sister and the king took her to be his wife anyway. But he let Abram live. And he also gave Abram sheep and goats and cattle and made him a very rich man. After all, the king thought Sarai was Abram's sister. But when he found out that Sarai was actually Abram's wife, he made Abram take Sarai, and everything he owned, and leave the country. Hagar knew all of this and tried to be compassionate to Sarai. Sarai could be irritable and hard to please, but Hagar usually looked past these moods. But Hagar felt that Sarai had gone too far this time.

Sarai made Hagar sleep with Abram, hoping that Hagar would get pregnant. But when the plan worked,

Sarai became more hateful toward Hagar. Hagar had taken all she could handle from Sarai. And Hagar found herself pregnant and on the run – away from Sarai and Abram – and not sure of where she was going.

Hagar hadn't gotten very far when she met an angel from God. As the angel spoke with her, Hagar realized there was no place for her to go where she would be safe – as a runaway – a pregnant runaway. She didn't have any food and she only had the clothes on her back. She didn't have any shelter or protection from wild animals, or from men who might see her traveling alone.

The angel reminded her that she was pregnant and would need a safe place to give birth to her child, a son. But this would only happen if she went back. And she would have other children – grandchildren and great grandchildren. But only if she went back.

Hagar made her decision. She would go back and face her problems. She knew it wouldn't be easy, but the problems she would have, wandering in the desert on her own, would be so much greater than what she experienced with Sarai. It would be difficult, but she was convinced that those problems wouldn't last forever. She was convinced that God was with her, problems and all, and that God would help her.

*****

Strength Affirmations

I can manage problems.
I will not allow problems to manage me.

*****

Your Story—Your Strength

In what areas of your life have you
or will you affirm these strengths?

_____

_____

_____

_____

_____

_____

_____

_____

_____

_____

_____

_____

_____

_____

_____

_____

_____

_____

_____

_____

_____

_____

SARAH

Inspired by Genesis 18:1-15

*****

The Scripture

"But Sarah denied, saying, "I did not laugh"; for she was afraid. He said, "Oh yes, you did laugh.""
Genesis 18:15

*****

Her Story

Sarah had been a wife since she was a young girl. And like every girl who became a wife, she assumed she would have children, especially sons. But becoming pregnant, for Sarah, was like catching the wind. She just wasn't able to do it.

Each year, Sarah hoped that *this* would be the year she and Abraham would have a son. But with each year that passed, Sarah remained childless. And each year that she remained childless, she grew more and more desperate, so desperate that she told her slave girl, Hagar, to sleep with Abraham, hoping that Hagar would become pregnant and Sarah could take Hagar's son as her own. Sarah carried her desperation for years – for decades – feeling broken, rejected and abandoned by God, and ostracized and rejected by her community. For decades, her days were filled with tears.

And now, here she was, 90 years old, and she had long since given up on having a son. She had cried her last tears many years earlier, settling into the resolve that

17

she would never have her heart's desire. She was no longer sad, but she wasn't happy either. Sadness was no longer in her heart, but neither was joy. That was so, until today.

Today she laughed. And why wouldn't she? She was told that God remembered her prayer. Just when she thought her body was dead, she heard a voice from God saying that she would give birth – that nine months from that date, she would be nursing a son. *And she laughed.* Just when she thought that life would never hold any meaning for her, she heard God's voice, reminding her that her request hadn't be forgotten. Joy exploded in her heart. *And she laughed.*

Sarah was 90 years old and her husband was nearly 100. In nine months, they would have a son. Oh yes! *She laughed.* And why wouldn't she? Her laughter was simply the *Amen* to a prayer she had prayed long, long ago.

*****

Strength Affirmations

I will cry. I will laugh. I will express every emotion
that God has given me, without fear, shame or apology.

*****

Your Story—Your Strength

In what areas of your life have you
or will you affirm these strengths?

_____

_____

_____

_____

_____

_____

_____

_____

_____

Kanisha L. Adkins

KETURAH

Inspired by Genesis 25:1-6

*****

The Scripture

"Abraham took another wife, whose name was Keturah." Genesis 25:1

*****

Her Story

Keturah knew there was a significant age difference between the two of them. But the age difference was the least of her concerns. Abraham wanted to take her as his wife, and she had a decision to make. He had been married before and he and his first wife Sarah, now deceased, had a son.

Keturah had sat for weeks, listening to Abraham's stories about Sarah; stories about his God, who had promised to bless him and Sarah with a son; stories about how it seemed this son would never be born; stories about how Sarah was *so* desperate to have a son that she told her slave-girl Hagar to sleep with Abraham, hoping that Hagar would become pregnant and Sarah could take Hagar's son as her own. Keturah listened to him talk about how he and Sarah were finally blessed with the birth of a son, Isaac, and how God had promised him that a great and powerful nation would descend from this son.

Keturah had listened to the stories for weeks. She wasn't quite sure if any of this would affect her when

21

Abraham said that he wanted to take her as his wife. What she was sure of was that he was able to take care of her and any children they might have. He was, after all, a very wealthy man.

She had no idea that he would leave most of his wealth to Isaac and would only give token gifts to her sons. She had no idea that he would send her sons away – sons she had had for him – away from Isaac, to live in another part of the country. This is what would happen in the future, and Keturah didn't know what the future would hold. But she considered everything he told her. She made her decision and she believed it was a wise decision. She agreed to be his wife.

*****

Strength Affirmations

I am responsible for my decisions. I am capable
of making thoughtful choices. My choices are
worthy of respect!

*****

Your Story—Your Strength

In what areas of your life have you
or will you affirm these strengths?

_____

_____

_____

_____

_____

_____

_____

_____

Kanisha L. Adkins

JUDITH, BASEMATH & REBEKAH

Inspired by Genesis 26:34-35

*****

The Scripture

"When Esau was forty years old, he married Judith daughter of Beeri the Hittite, and Basemath daughter of Elon the Hittite;" Genesis 26:34

*****

Her Story

Judith and Basemath were very much alike. They were both Hittites, born in Canaan. They both had close-knit families who spent most of their work and leisure time together. And like most girls, they wanted husbands.

Esau wasn't from Canaan and he wasn't a Hittite. He knew that some of his family's traditions and beliefs were different from Judith and Basemath's but *he chose them anyway*. He spoke with their fathers and was given permission to take them as his wives.

After taking them as his wives, Judith and Basemath went to live with Esau and his family. And as part of his family, they did their share of work, just as they had done in their fathers' houses. And even though Esau and his parents, Isaac and Rebekah, were descendants of immigrants who had come to Canaan from another country, Judith and Basemath treated them with respect. But in spite of the respect shown to them, Isaac and Rebekah didn't show respect to Judith and Basemath – because they were Canaanite women!

Judith and Basemath noticed that their very presence seemed to sicken Isaac and Rebekah. The two women often talked to each other, trying to figure out why Isaac and Rebekah had such contempt for Canaanites. Was it the color of their skin? Was it the texture of their hair or their physical features? Was it the foods they ate or the way they worshiped? Maybe Isaac and Rebekah regretted leaving their home and family and felt out of place in Canaan.

It was a mystery that the women couldn't figure out. And after years of trying to figure out their crime, they decided that *there was no crime*. In *their* eyes, they were descendants of hard-working, devoted and devout people. In some ways, they may have been different from their husband's parents and his extended family, but they had always been respectful. They wanted this same respect shown to them. But even without it, they wouldn't change. They would be who they had always been and they saw no reason to change.

*****

Strength Affirmations

I respect differences and I appreciate diversity.
My personal contributions and unique personality
outweigh all negative stereotypes.

*****

Your Story—Your Strength

In what areas of your life have you
or will you affirm these strengths?

_____

_____

_____

_____

_____

_____

_____

_____

MAHALATH

Inspired by Genesis 27:46 - 28:8-9

*****

The Scripture

"Esau went to Ishmael and took Mahalath daughter of Abraham's son Ishmael, and sister of Nebaioth, to be his wife in addition to the wives he had." Genesis 28:9

*****

Her Story

After Mahalath became Esau's wife, she left her family to live with him and his family. When Mahalath arrived in Canaan where Esau lived, his parents, Isaac and Rebekah, welcomed her into their family from the moment they met her. Rebekah, in particular, treated Mahalath like her very own daughter. And Mahalath soon found her place in the family.

She had a good relationship with Esau's other wives, Judith and Basemath. Judith and Basemath were Hittite and had lived in Canaan all of their lives. They embraced Mahalath and helped her get used to her new surroundings and the culture. She was grateful to them. And she had a great deal of respect for Isaac and Rebekah. Mahalath had a caring, peaceful relationship with all of her new family. But she noticed that Isaac, and particularly Rebekah, seemed to be offended with Judith and Basemath.

Mahalath noticed that Rebekah seldom engaged in conversation with them and when she did, she was extremely rude. She noticed that Rebekah rarely offered to help them with household chores. And she was sure that she had overheard Rebekah complaining to Isaac, on more than one occasion, about how *disgusted* she was with having to live in the same town as Hittite women. Mahalath had even seen Rebekah become ill because of how much she detested Judith and Basemath. It wasn't pleasant when Rebekah was alone with Judith and Basemath, but when Mahalath was with them, all of Rebekah's ill-feelings seemed to fade away.

And so, Mahalath made a point of trying to make life better for Judith and Basemath. She had compassion on them because she remembered the stories her grandmother Hagar told her. Stories of how Hagar was taken away from her family as a young girl. Stories of how the family that took her in ultimately mistreated and abused her. Stories of how they made her a slave, made her sleep with her master, and then put her out after she became pregnant by him and had his son.

Mahalath had seen how the mistreatment and rejection affected her grandmother. Judith and Basemath were rejected just like her grandmother. But she, Mahalath, was the wife who was acceptable to Esau's parents. She was the wife who lifted Rebekah's spirits and who helped ease the tension and ill-feelings Rebekah had towards Judith and Basemath. When Mahalath arrived in Canaan, she thought she was simply one of Esau's wives. She didn't realize how important she would be to the whole family. She was the one who brought peace to a family in chaos.

Strength Affirmations

My purpose is to bring peace and order.
My presence makes life better.

*****

Your Story—Your Strength

In what areas of your life have you
or will you affirm these strengths?

_____

_____

_____

_____

_____

_____

_____

_____

Kanisha L. Adkins

LEAH

Inspired by Genesis 29

*****

The Scripture

"Leah's eyes were lovely, and Rachel was graceful and beautiful." Genesis 29:17

*****

Her Story

Leah was beautiful but she didn't think so. She was physically attractive with a beautiful spirit. But she was self-conscious because of a condition with her eyes that made them sensitive to light. She may not have been able to see her own beauty, but she had no problem seeing the beauty in others, particularly a young man named Jacob whom her father hired as a shepherd. Leah didn't have a husband and she thought maybe her father would arrange for her to be Jacob's wife. Jacob was nice to Leah, but it was obvious that he preferred to spend time with her younger sister Rachel.

Several years later, Leah's wish came true. Her father, Laban, gave her to Jacob to be his wife. But something was wrong. A few days after becoming Jacob's wife, she overheard him arguing with Laban, accusing him of being deceptive. He said that he had agreed to work for Laban in exchange for Rachel, not Leah. She heard Laban tell Jacob it was his people's custom that the oldest daughter would get married before the youngest daughter. And then she heard Laban agree to give Rachel to be Jacob's wife if Jacob would agree to work for Laban seven more years. Leah was devastated! Seven years later, Rachel became Jacob's wife. As time went by, Leah tried to convince herself that everything was fine and that Jacob loved her. But she could see that Jacob loved Rachel more.

When Leah became pregnant and gave birth to their first son, she was *sure* Jacob would love her more. But she was wrong. When she had their second son, she thought this might change Jacob's feelings for her, but it didn't. Neither did the birth of their third son. The more she hoped for his love, the more she noticed that he loved Rachel. For years, Leah was heart-broken, wanting Jacob to love her and hoping that she could earn his love with the birth of another child.

After years of depression and desperation, something happened. She became pregnant and gave birth to their fourth son. But this time was different. Suddenly, she no longer felt desperate for Jacob's love or validation. She finally realized that the birth of each child was God's way of saying, "I see you and I love you." And as she looked at her fourth son, Judah, instead of pining over Jacob, she praised God.

*****

Strength Affirmations

I was created in the image of God and I am beautiful.
I have God's attention. I am worthy of God's love!

*****

Your Story—Your Strength

In what areas of your life have you
or will you affirm these strengths?

_____

_____

_____

_____

_____

_____

_____

_____

Kanisha L. Adkins

_____

_____

_____

_____

_____

_____

_____

_____

_____

_____

_____

_____

_____

RACHEL

Inspired by Genesis 29

*****

The Scripture

"While he was still speaking with them, Rachel came with her father's sheep; for she kept them."
Genesis 29:9

*****

Her Story

Rachel lived the life of a shepherd. Like all of the other shepherds, she had to get up early in the morning and lead the sheep and goats out of the fold to a place where they could graze and eat. She had a large flock and would often walk for miles to find a place that had enough grass where they could graze. When the season changed and the grassy areas dried up, Rachel would hunt for leafy bushes and soft twigs to feed the flock.

The rays of the sun could be brutal as the day went on, so she was often searching for shade where the flock could escape the heat. Occasionally a sheep or goat would wander away and Rachel would look for it and bring it back to the flock.

It wasn't unusual for her to walk for several hours, leading her flock to a quiet stream so that they could be watered. When the flock came to water that had to be crossed, Rachel would lead the way, making sure each animal made it to the other side. When a little lamb was afraid to cross a stream, Rachel would pick up the lamb and carry it safely to the other side. When one of the goats had an injured leg, Rachel cleaned the wound and rubbed it with healing oils and herbs.

Even though Rachel was more than capable of taking care of her flock, the male shepherds helped her with some of the more strenuous jobs – like moving the stones away from the opening of the wells that were used to water the flocks. The men had to roll the stones away so that they could water their flocks, too. But whenever Rachel was nearby, it was obvious that the men wanted to impress her with their strength. That's because Rachel was an attractive young lady. She had a pretty face and a beautiful figure. Men were drawn to her because of her physical beauty. But there was more to her than this. She was a woman who worked hard to help provide for her family. It was her responsibility to take care of the flock and her job wasn't any less demanding simply because she was a beautiful woman.

*****

Strength Affirmations

I am hard-working and productive.
My work has value.

*****

Your Story—Your Strength

In what areas of your life have you
or will you affirm these strengths?

_____

_____

_____

_____

_____

_____

_____

_____

_____

Kanisha L. Adkins

BILHAH & ZILPAH

Inspired by Genesis 30:1-13

*****

The Scripture

"And Bilhah conceived and bore Jacob a son."
Genesis 30:5

"Then Leah's maid Zilpah bore Jacob a son."
Genesis 30:10

*****

Her Story

Bilhah and Zilpah were born into a time and place where they had no choice on how they would live their lives. All of their lives they had been Laban's slaves. When Laban's daughter Leah got married, Laban gave Zilpah to her as a wedding gift. A few years later, when Rachel got married, Laban gave Bilhah to her as a wedding gift. Zilpah and Bilhah thought life might have gotten easier for them, working for the women instead of their father. But they were wrong. The worst of it started after Leah had four sons.

Rachel was jealous because she didn't have any children. She was so desperate that she gave Bilhah to her husband, hoping that Bilhah would get pregnant. Rachel's plan worked, twice, and each time, she took Bilhah's son and became his mother. Then Leah became jealous of Rachel and she gave Zilpah to her husband hoping the same thing would happen. Leah's plan worked. Zilpah became pregnant, twice, and Leah took the babies from her and became their mother.

Bilhah and Zilpah agonized that the children would never be considered theirs. But in their hearts, the babies were theirs. When the babies were hungry, they were the ones who nursed them. When the babies were sick, they were the ones who cared for them. And when the babies cried, they were the ones who held them. Bilhah and Zilpah pretended not to care, but their hearts ached and they grieved every time the babies were taken from their arms.

Bilhah and Zilpah didn't dare let their mistresses know their true feelings. But each understood what the other was going through. And when Rachel and Leah were out of sight, Bilhah and Zilpah wept. They gave each other permission to grieve. They grieved every loss they had experienced – the loss of their babies, the loss of their choices, the loss of the lives that they might have lived.

*****

Strength Affirmations

I will acknowledge my pain. I will give myself time
and space to mourn my losses.

*****

Your Story—Your Strength

In what areas of your life have you
or will you affirm these strengths?

_____

_____

_____

_____

_____

_____

_____

_____

_____

Kanisha L. Adkins

DINAH

Inspired by Genesis 34

*****

The Scripture

"Now Dinah the daughter of Leah, whom she had borne to Jacob, went out to visit the women of the region. When Shechem son of Hamor the Hivite, prince of the region, saw her, he seized her and lay with her by force." Genesis 34:1-2

*****

Her Story

Dinah was the only girl in a family of eleven boys. Dinah's brothers thought the world of their sister and they were very protective of her. But even though she was the only girl, she wasn't lost or overlooked in such a large family. She was outgoing and outspoken and she could hold her own with her brothers and with most people. When Dinah and her family moved to Canaan, she decided to go out one day to meet some of the ladies who lived in the city.

While Dinah was on her way, a group of men noticed her. After she passed them, one of the men came behind Dinah, put one hand over her mouth and, with the other, dragged her off the well-traveled road to a secluded place in the trees. Dinah kicked, punched, scratched and tried to push him away, but he overpowered and raped her. When Dinah was finally able to get away from him, she ran home, frightened and hysterical, crying to her family.

45

Dinah's father, Jacob, sent one of his servants to the fields where her brothers were working to tell them what happened. The brothers were furious and immediately left work, without finishing their jobs. When they arrived home, Shechem, the man who raped Dinah, and Hamor, his father, were there, making Jacob an offer: Hamor would give Jacob his daughters in return for Jacob giving Dinah to Shechem as his wife. Hamor also said that Jacob and his family could share the land and their families would blend together.

Dinah's brothers were furious. Shechem had treated their sister like a piece of trash. And now, he was asking to have her as his wife, never once mentioning the horrible thing he had done to her. They vowed to each other that they would punish Shechem and his entire household. And they promised Dinah that they would not add insult to injury by making her live as Shechem's wife.

Jacob gave Dinah to Shechem on the condition that Shechem, Hamor and all of the men of their city would agree to be circumcised, which was one of the Israelites' religious customs. Shechem and Hamor agreed. All of the men of their city were circumcised. Shechem and Hamor thought they were now allies and friends with Jacob and his family, and that Shechem had Dinah as his wife.

But on the third day, while the men were still weak with pain from the circumcisions, two of Dinah's brothers, Simeon and Levi, ambushed the city and killed all of the men. And Dinah, who had refused to be abused and remain silent, was rescued and returned home to her family.

Strength Affirmations

I will speak the truth if I am abused. I will not be silent if I am mistreated.

*****

Your Story—Your Strength

In what areas of your life have you
or will you affirm these strengths?

_____

_____

_____

_____

_____

_____

_____

_____

_____

Kanisha L. Adkins

TAMAR

Inspired by Genesis 38:1-26

*****

The Scripture

"Judah said to his daughter-in-law Tamar, "Stay as a widow in your father's household until my son Shelah grows up." He thought Shelah would die like his brothers had. So Tamar went and lived in her father's household." Genesis 38:11

*****

Her Story

Tamar was still a young girl when she married Er. But they never had children because Er died, not long after they married. Tamar's father-in-law, Judah, arranged for his son Onan to be a type of surrogate on behalf of Er. It was a family tradition – if a son died without children, a male surrogate would be used to have a child on behalf of the deceased son with his widow. The deceased son would have descendants and the wife would remain part of her husband's family.

Onan reluctantly obeyed his father because he knew that the child wouldn't be considered his. So, Onan was intimate with Tamar but he purposefully tried to make sure that she wouldn't become pregnant. And his plan worked. He didn't have children for his brother, Er.

Judah had one son left, Shelah, but he wasn't old enough to have a wife. Judah promised Tamar that as soon as Shelah was old enough, he would be a surrogate and Tamar would remain a part of their family. In the meantime, Judah sent Tamar back to her father's house to wait. Years passed while Tamar waited, but Judah never came to get her.

One day, Tamar heard that Judah was coming to the area where she lived to take care of some business. She decided to meet and confront him about not keeping his promise. When Judah saw Tamar, he didn't recognize her because she had a veil over her face. Before she could confront him, he propositioned her: if she would sleep with him, he would send her one of the animals from his flock. Tamar asked him for a guarantee, a type of security deposit, that he would send the animal. He gave her his seal, cord and staff which were unique to him. Tamar agreed. When he sent her the animal, she would send the seal, cord and staff back to him.

Several months later, Judah received a message that his daughter-in-law Tamar had become a prostitute and that she was now pregnant. Judah ordered that she be brought to him and burned. When Tamar came to him, he was in for a shock. She was pregnant – by the man who had left the seal, cord and staff that she had in her possession. Judah recognized the items. They belonged to him! And he confessed that Tamar wasn't a sinful woman, that she was actually more righteous than he was because he failed to keep his promise to Tamar. But Tamar had honored her commitment to be reunited back with her husband's family.

Strength Affirmations

I am loyal to my commitments. I will work for what I rightfully deserve. I will patiently wait to receive what has been promised to me.

*****

Your Story—Your Strength

In what areas of your life have you or will you affirm these strengths?

_____

_____

_____

_____

_____

_____

_____

_____

_____

_____

_____

_____

_____

_____

_____

_____

_____

_____

_____

_____

ASENATH

Inspired by Genesis 41:39-54

*****

The Scripture

"Before the years of famine came, Joseph had two sons, whom Asenath daughter of Potiphera, priest of On, bore to him." Genesis 41:50

*****

Her Story

When Asenath became Joseph's wife, all of the women envied her. Joseph was talented, handsome, well-built and one of the most powerful men in Egypt, second only to the king. Nothing was done in Egypt unless Joseph approved it. The women thought Asenath had everything a woman could possibly want. But what they didn't know is that along with all of the glory, there was a lot of grief because Joseph had a past that was filled with pain. And when Asenath became his wife, Joseph's pain became her pain.

Asenath knew Joseph's painful story. *He had been born into a large family, at least ten half-brothers and one half-sister. He was the only child born to his mother Rachel and his father Jacob. And in spite of their large family, Joseph was Jacob's favorite, but his brothers resented him.*

Joseph's brothers hated him so much that, one day, when they were working in a field away from their father, they threw Joseph into a pit, then sat down to

53

eat lunch while trying to decide whether they would kill him. Instead, they sold him to a group of men who were passing by.

The salesmen sold him to a man named Potiphar, the chief guard for the king of Egypt. Joseph was enslaved to Potiphar for over ten years. To add to his misery and misfortune, he was accused of trying to sleep with Potiphar's wife and put in prison.

Eventually, the king released him from prison and made him second in command over all the people of Egypt. In spite of his new position and power, Joseph was still haunted by his past.

This was the man that Asenath married. But Asenath gave him new life and new hope. When she gave birth to their first son, Joseph named him Manasseh, which means "God has made me fruitful in the land of my suffering." And when she gave birth to their second son, Joseph named him Ephraim, which means "God has given me children in the land where I've been treated harshly."

The king of Egypt had promoted Joseph to a position of prestige and power and the promise of a bright future. But it was *Asenath* who helped him recover from a painful past.

Strength Affirmations

I can create a vibrant future in spite of a harsh history. I can give hope to people who are suffering.

*****

Your Story—Your Strength

In what areas of your life have you
or will you affirm these strengths?

_____

_____

_____

_____

_____

_____

_____

_____

_____

SHIPHRAH & PUAH

Inspired by Exodus 1:8-21

*****

The Scripture

"The king of Egypt spoke to two Hebrew midwives named Shiphrah and Puah: "When you are helping the Hebrew women give birth and you see the baby being born, if it's a boy, kill him. But if it's a girl, you can let her live."" Exodus 1:15-16

*****

Her Story

Shiphrah and Puah served as midwives in the community where they lived. The midwives were responsible for helping hundreds of women bring new life into the world. They were compassionate with the mothers and gentle with the babies. They believed each baby was a gift from God. And after each child was delivered, they continued to assist the mothers with caring for their children. Shiphrah and Puah absolutely adored children. But they found themselves in a terrible predicament when they were ordered by the king of Egypt to kill all of the male babies born to Hebrew women.

Shiphrah and Puah refused to obey. They continued to bring life into the world. They delivered girls *and boys*, and safely placed each baby – alive and well – into its mother's arms. They disobeyed the king, knowing that they were putting their own lives at stake. Weeks and months went by with Shiphrah and Puah delivering healthy, happy babies – girls *and* boys – until one day they were told that the king wanted to see them. Shiphrah and Puah knew then that the king had heard they were allowing the Hebrew boys to live after the mothers had given birth to them. The two women had known this day would come and they were ready.

When the king asked them why they were disobeying him, they lied! They knew the king was a powerful man, but they knew he was also not a very knowledgeable man. He knew *nothing* about pregnancy and childbirth, not to mention that there was no difference between how Hebrew and Egyptian women gave birth. So, they told him that the Hebrew women were very strong, unlike the Egyptian women. They told him by the time they arrived to help deliver the babies, the mothers had already given birth – and he believed them!

Shiphrah and Puah were relieved that the king didn't punish them. Of course, he was still afraid that the Hebrew men would increase in numbers and eventually take over Egypt. He would have to think of another way to limit the number of Hebrew males. But while he was focused on death and dying, Shiphrah and Puah were focused on life and living.

*****

Strength Affirmations

I am committed to life and living. I will not be controlled by anyone's insecurities or fears, including my own.

*****

Your Story—Your Strength

In what areas of your life have you or will you affirm these strengths?

_____

_____

_____

_____

_____

_____

_____

_____

_____

_____

Kanisha L. Adkins

JOCHEBED

Inspired by Exodus 2:1-10

*****

The Scripture

*****

"The name of Amram's wife was Jochebed daughter of Levi, who was born to Levi in Egypt; and she bore to Amram: Aaron, Moses, and their sister Miriam." Number 26:59

*****

Her Story

Jochebed was no stranger to what it meant to honor God. As a young girl, she had been told the stories of how her great, great grandmother Sarah (and great, great grandfather Abraham) had an encounter with God who had promised to bless them and all of their descendants. Because of this promise, God deserved *all* honor, over and above all other gods and people. This lesson was etched in Jochebed's heart. Years later, this lesson and her heart would be tested.

While living in Egypt, Jochebed married a man named Amram, another Israelite, and they had two children, Miriam and Aaron. The small group of Israelite people who had migrated to Egypt had multiplied and grown so large in numbers that they far exceeded the number of Egyptian people. The king of Egypt, fearing that the Israelites would take over Egypt, tried to stop their growth by ordering that all of the male babies born to the Israelite women be drowned.

But Jochebed remembered that God was to be honored above all. And when she and Amram had their third child, *a boy*, she hid him for three months. When the baby became too large to hide, Jochebed spoke with her husband, Amram. She pleaded with him to help her protect their son. Amram felt helpless against the king's command. But Jochebed was determined to honor God. She refused to drown the baby.

Instead, she placed the baby in a basket made of straw reeds and covered it with tar to keep the water, fish and reptiles out. She put the basket near the riverbank, praying that someone would see it floating and would take pity on her baby boy. Jochebed defied the king's orders and honored her God. And in turn, God honored her faith, answered her prayer and delivered her son back into her arms.

*****

Strength Affirmations

I will honor the spirit of the Creator above all others!
I will use my creativity to preserve life and build my future.

*****

Your Story—Your Strength

In what areas of your life have you
or will you affirm these strengths?

_____

_____

_____

_____

_____

_____

_____

_____

ZIPPORAH

Inspired by Exodus 4:18-26

*****

The Scripture

"But Zipporah took a flint and cut off her son's foreskin, and touched Moses' feet with it, and said, "Truly you are a bridegroom of blood to me!"" Exodus 4:25

*****

Her Story

Zipporah and her husband gathered their belongings and their son, Gershom, and started on their trip from Midian to Egypt. Zipporah thought they were going to Egypt so that her husband could check on his family. That's what he had told her father. She thought he would be happy and excited to see his family. But as they walked, Zipporah noticed that Moses, her husband, was trembling and sweating profusely and that he couldn't catch his breath. He insisted that he was fine but Zipporah insisted that they stop to rest for a few minutes. That's when Moses told Zipporah about his visit from God.

God had instructed him to return to Egypt to order the king of Egypt to release the Hebrew people from slavery. Moses had given excuse after excuse as to why he couldn't follow God's instructions. Zipporah thought that, maybe, this was why he was so ill. He was terrified of the assignment that had been given to him. He was afraid they might reject him because he had never been enslaved and he had never experienced the suffering they had experienced.

65

But there was one more thing. Hebrew traditions required all Hebrew boys to be circumcised and Moses hadn't circumcised Gershom. He was afraid they might reject him for not honoring this tradition.

Zipporah couldn't believe what she was hearing! Moses was taking her and their son into a potentially deadly situation. There was no telling how the king of Egypt or the Hebrew people would treat them. Zipporah had no control over what would happen with the king. But she had to make sure that the Hebrew people would embrace her son as one of their own.

Zipporah knew what had to be done. And as she looked at Moses, lying on the ground and unable to move, she knew that *she* had to do it. Zipporah prepared a solution of water and herbs and gave it to her son to drink. (As shepherds, she and her sisters had often used the herbs to calm a sheep when it became wounded or hurt and they needed to clean and dress its wound.) She hoped the herbs would calm Gershom. When she saw that he was falling asleep, Zipporah took a deep breath, grabbed a sharp stone – her hands shaking over the thought of hurting her own child – and she swiftly cut the foreskin from her young son's genitals.

Semi-conscious, Gershom screamed and began to cry. Zipporah was crying too. She was crying because she was angry about what she had been forced to do to her son. She threw the skin at Moses and rubbed the blood all over him. *He had played a part in this too. Their son's blood was on him too.* Then she picked up her son to comfort him. And she was comforted by the fact that she had been able to save her husband and her son's lives.

Strength Affirmations

I am courageous. I am capable of doing what others refuse to do. I will fight to save the lives of the people I love.

*****

Your Story—Your Strength

In what areas of your life have you
or will you affirm these strengths?

_____

_____

_____

_____

_____

_____

_____

_____

_____

Kanisha L. Adkins

ELISHEBA

Inspired by Exodus 6:23

*****

The Scripture

"Aaron married Elisheba, daughter of Amminadab and sister of Nahshon, and she bore him Nadab, Abihu, Eleazar, and Ithamar." Exodus 6:23

*****

Her Story

Everyone who knew Elisheba wondered if she was one of God's prophets. It was obvious that she lived her life, from childhood through adulthood, aware of the power and presence of God. As a young girl, she had been taught about God's love for her distant grandmother, Leah. She heard the stories of her grandmother's heartache when she realized that her husband didn't love her but instead loved her sister. She heard about her grandmother's pain over not being able to have children and how, out of desperation, she made her female slave sleep with her husband so that she could claim the children as her own. She heard that her grandmother was finally able to become pregnant and that with the birth of each child, grandmother Leah kept clinging to the hope that her husband would love her.

Elisheba had heard the stories hundreds of times. But the part of the stories that meant the most to Elisheba was when grandmother Leah had her fourth son. *That* was when grandmother Leah realized how much her God loved her. *That* was when she stopped feeling desperate for her husband's love and instead, started giving praise for God's love.

Embracing and showing God's love was central to Elisheba's life. So, it was no surprise that a man from the tribe of Levi chose her to be his wife. And it was no surprise that she passed her deep devotion to God along to her sons.

Her husband was a prophet and a high priest. He was responsible for teaching the people of Israel the laws of God, for taking care of the sanctuary and its sacred objects, and for teaching the men who assisted him the functions they were to perform. Elisheba's sons – Nadab, Abihu, Eleazar and Ithamar – were also priests. They worked with their father, taking care of the sanctuary and the sacred objects.

Neighbors, family and friends often spoke to each other, and to Elisheba, about her family's dedicated service to God. Even her brother-in-law and sister-in-law were prophets for God, and people couldn't help but wonder if Elisheba might also be a prophet. They had suggested it to her throughout her life.

Elisheba, however, never claimed to be a prophet. Aside from the suggestions of family and friends, Elisheba never gave it much thought. Being a prophet was an honorable calling – one which she respected. But for Elisheba, her dedication and service to her people was grounded in love: God's love for her and her love for God.

Strength Affirmations

I am called to love God and to love God's people.
Love is my highest calling.

*****

Your Story—Your Strength

In what areas of your life have you
or will you affirm these strengths?

_____

_____

_____

_____

_____

_____

_____

_____

_____

Kanisha L. Adkins

SHELOMITH

Inspired by Leviticus 24:10-23

*****

The Scripture

"The Israelite woman's son blasphemed the Name in a curse. And they brought him to Moses—now his mother's name was Shelomith, daughter of Dibri, of the tribe of Dan." Leviticus 24:11

*****

Her Story

Shelomith was a peaceful woman, but the same couldn't be said about many of her family. She was a descendant from the tribe of Dan. Many of them were known for being argumentative and disruptive. And it wasn't unusual for some of the men to get into fights. On this day, it was Shelomith's son who got into a fight with another Israelite. The women sent for Shelomith to see if she could stop her son and somehow bring peace between the two men. But by the time she arrived it was too late. Her son had been arrested and jailed. His crime? He had used *The Name* of God carelessly. The religious practices of the people of Israel strictly prohibited saying the sacred name of God, except during religious ceremonies.

Shelomith spoke with the Israelite man with whom her son fought. She found out what the dispute was about and she settled it. But settling their disagreement was minor. That's because everyone who saw the fight had also heard her son say *The Name* of God. And Shelomith wasn't sure that she could save her son from being punished. But she would try.

She spoke to the judge in an effort to convince him to release her son. She pleaded, explaining that he was still young and, like many of the young men, was easily offended and didn't always make wise decisions. She tried to remain calm, but the peace that she normally felt quickly faded away as the judge refused to accommodate her request. She learned that her son wouldn't be released. He would be punished. And for his punishment, he would be held down and stoned to death by everyone who heard him say *The Name*. He would be made an example of what happens to those who disrespect *The Name* of God.

At that moment, Shelomith's peaceful world spun out of control. She started to lose consciousness and felt as if she were sinking into a dark hole with no air to breathe. Just when she thought she had taken her last breath, she was startled back to consciousness by the screams and cries of a woman lying on the ground near the crowd who would kill her son. She realized that *she* was that woman, screaming and crying, with no memory of the peace she had carried in her heart just hours ago. She was the one that people had called on to bring peace into their chaotic lives. Now, she would spend days, weeks, months and maybe even years, searching for her own peace.

Strength Affirmations

I am committed to mercy, justice and peace.
I give myself permission to grieve what has been
taken from me.

*****

Your Story—Your Strength

In what areas of your life have you
or will you affirm these strengths?

_____

_____

_____

_____

_____

_____

_____

_____

_____

Kanisha L. Adkins

MIRIAM

Inspired by Numbers 12

*****

The Scripture

"So Miriam was shut out of the camp for seven days; and the people did not set out on the march until Miriam had been brought in again." Numbers 12:15

*****

Her Story

Miriam was one of the most gifted women among her people, the Israelites. She was able to move people to celebrate, especially to praise and worship God. When she and the Israelites left Egypt, marched on dry ground through the Red Sea and reached the desert of Shur, Miriam picked up her tambourine and started to dance and sing. Miriam was so passionate in her praise, that the people couldn't help but join her. The women followed her lead and started to dance and play tambourines. Then the men and children joined in the celebration. They had all escaped Pharaoh and his army, untouched and unharmed.

But Miriam wasn't just a gifted worshiper. She was one of God's mighty prophets. She often spoke to the Israelites on God's behalf. God spoke to her in dreams and visions. And she would give the people instructions so that they could live in a way that was pleasing to God. All of the people, men, women and children, recognized Miriam's gift as a prophet. Even her brothers, Moses and Aaron, recognized her gifts. Moses and Aaron were also prophets and the three of them had a very close relationship with each other. But Miriam and Aaron had one problem with their brother: Moses had married a woman from Cush. And because he had married a woman from Cush, Miriam and Aaron began to complain about Moses's leadership.

They felt that some of his decisions may not have been in the best interest of Israel – maybe even that his loyalties were divided between his Cushite wife and the people of Israel. After all, they were prophets who heard from God, too. And so, while the Israelites were still camped in Hazeroth, Miriam and Aaron decided to remind Moses that he was not the only prophet among the people of Israel.

Then the strangest thing happened. Miriam and Aaron had *both* complained about Moses's Cushite wife. They had *both* challenged Moses with the fact that he wasn't Israel's only prophet – they were prophets too! God had become angry with both of them. And they were *both* terrified, but *Miriam* was the only one whom God seemed to punish. Because only Miriam's skin started to flake off and turn white.

When Aaron saw Miriam's skin, he became even more terrified. He thought the same thing might happen to him because he had been just as disrespectful to Moses as Miriam had been. So Aaron begged and pleaded with Moses, and Moses begged and pleaded with God to heal Miriam.

God agreed to heal Miriam, but the Israelites' laws required her to be quarantined for seven days so that no one else would become sick. And even though the Israelites had made plans to leave Hazeroth before Miriam became sick, they refused to leave until she was healed and able to travel, because she was one of God's prophets and they valued her and her gifts.

*****

Strength Affirmations

I am part of a community that loves me and welcomes my gifts. My gifts add value to the community.

*****

Your Story—Your Strength

In what areas of your life have you
or will you affirm these strengths?

_____

_____

_____

_____

_____

_____

_____

_____

_____

COZBI

Inspired by Numbers 25:1-15

*****

The Scripture

"The name of the Midianite woman who was killed was Cozbi daughter of Zur, who was the head of a clan, an ancestral house in Midian." Numbers 25:15

*****

Her Story

Cozbi had gone to her wedding tent with her new husband, Zimri. As she approached the tent, she noticed many of the Israelite people sitting at a tent across from hers and crying. Zimri told her they were in mourning because some of the Israelite men had slept with Moabite women and had worshiped Moabite gods. The Israelites believed this was why so many of their people were sick and dying. Zimri, also an Israelite, hadn't participated in any type of relationship with the Moabite women. He had taken Cozbi, a Midianite woman, as his wife – just as Moses had taken a Midianite wife, Zipporah.

Cozbi and Zimri had only been in their tent a few minutes when a man with a spear ran into the tent and stabbed Zimri to death. Cozbi sat horrified, unable to move. An even if she *could* move, there was no point in trying to run because she would never be able to get away. She looked at her husband and at the man who had just killed him. She reached for Zimri, who was gasping for breath, and she managed to ask, "Why?", not really expecting an answer.

The man with the spear was in a rage, not really responding to Cozbi's question, but yelling and screaming, "All Moabite women must die so that Israel can be saved from this horrible disease." Cozbi's thoughts were spinning and she was going into shock. She was trying to understand why her husband had been killed and what this madman was talking about when she felt the excruciating pain of the spear being plunged into her belly, all while the deranged man kept yelling insults about Moabite women.

The terrible ordeal only lasted for seconds, but as Cozbi lay dying, it seemed to last forever. And as she took her last few breaths, she realized that she had been wrongfully accused and then sacrificed like an animal because of someone else's wrongdoing.

*****

Strength Affirmations

I am blameless against the bad behaviors
and prejudices of other people.

*****

Your Story—Your Strength

In what areas of your life have you
or will you affirm these strengths?

_____

_____

_____

_____

_____

_____

_____

_____

Kanisha L. Adkins

SERAH

Inspired by Numbers 26

*****

The Scripture

"And the name of the daughter of Asher was Serah."
Numbers 26:46

*****

Her Story

Serah was one of just a few women in a family that valued men more than it valued women. She never knew her mother but she knew her grandmother's name was Zilpah (and her grandfather's name was Israel). She had several brothers and eleven uncles. She had no sisters, but she had an aunt, Dinah, whom she adored. Every time one of her uncles had a child, more times than not, the child always seemed to be a boy. And even when a girl was born, little attention was given to her.

Most of the attention was focused on the boys and the men – what kind of work they should do, what kind of women they should marry, how much land they would be given to take care of their families, and what they would inherit when their fathers died. Serah *never* heard her father or grandfather talk about her future. But she made up in her mind that she *would* have a future – even when she was disregarded by the majority of people around her or given what was left over.

Serah was seen but seldom heard. When everyone else was busy talking, Serah was busy listening. When everyone else was busy trying to show how much they knew, Serah was busy learning. When everyone else was given the first and the best, Serah took the leftovers and made them into something that would last.

Serah lived a long life because of her determination and strength. She was able to find a place for herself and make her presence known within a family that preferred men. Serah could have been left out, but she persisted and made a name for herself. Her place and presence were so significant that she was named among the warriors of the children of Israel and she was named among those who would receive an inheritance as descendants of Israel.

*****

Strength Affirmations

I am significant and I will be acknowledged.
I will build a legacy that lasts.

*****

Your Story—Your Strength

In what areas of your life have you
or will you affirm these strengths?

_____

_____

_____

_____

_____

_____

_____

_____

_____

MAHLAH, NOAH, HOGLAH, MILCAH & TIRZAH

Inspired by Numbers 26:52-56; 27:1-8

*****

The Scripture

"Then the daughters of Zelophehad came forward. Zelophehad was son of Hepher son of Gilead son of Machir son of Manasseh son of Joseph, a member of the Manassite clans. The names of his daughters were: Mahlah, Noah, Hoglah, Milcah, and Tirzah."
Numbers 27:1

*****

Her Story

*T*he sisters, Mahlah, Noah, Hoglah, Milcah and Tirzah, had listened for several months as the Israelites took their *second* census. The *first* census had been taken years earlier, before the Israelites crossed the desert at Sinai. By the time they reached Moab, all of the leaders who had been appointed before they started their journey had died. *The sisters'* father, Zelophehad, was among those who died in the desert. Now that the Israelites had reached the plains of Moab, *a second* census had to be taken. The census would be used to divide the land among the various families of the tribes of Israel and the land would be given to the male leaders of the families.

The sisters, were part of the tribe of Manasseh, one of the tribes designated to receive land. But because their father was deceased and they had no brothers, and because they were not married, the sisters were faced with being left out of the land distribution system.

But rather than allowing the system to leave them out, the sisters decided to do something that had never been done. They decided to change the system. *The sisters* stepped forward and spoke for themselves. They told the entire congregation that it would be unjust to act as if their father hadn't existed simply because he didn't have a son. They stated that their father's brothers would be given property. And they declared that they expected to be given property as well.

Everyone was in awe that *the sisters* dared to speak with such authority – in public – to male leaders. The men in the community rose up as if they would attack *the sisters*. The women hung their heads in fear and shame. *But God* spoke to Moses, the leader of the community, and said that *the sisters* were right. They were to be given property as an inheritance, just as their father's brothers would be given property. And God ordered Moses to change the system so that if a man died without sons, his property was to be given to his daughters.

*****

Strength Affirmations

I am my best advocate. I can defend my rights.
I am a trailblazer.

*****

Your Story—Your Strength

In what areas of your life have you
or will you affirm these strengths?

_____

_____

_____

_____

_____

_____

_____

_____

_____

_____

_____

_____

_____

_____

_____

_____

_____

_____

_____

_____

_____

RAHAB

Inspired by Joshua 2:1-14

*****

The Scripture

"But Rahab the prostitute, with her family and all who belonged to her, Joshua spared. Her family has lived in Israel ever since. For she hid the messengers whom Joshua sent to spy out Jericho." Joshua 6:25

*****

Her Story

Her name was Rahab. But no one ever referred to her as just Rahab. It was always Rahab the harlot or *Rahab the prostitute*. And there was good reason for why she was called Rahab the prostitute. She earned money and favors by having sex with men who lived in and visited the city of Jericho. She couldn't deny it. She *wouldn't* deny it. Prostitution was how she earned her living and how she supported her family.

But Rahab wasn't just a prostitute. She was a businesswoman. She made it her business to know what was going on in and outside of Jericho. She made it her business to know who lived in Jericho and who was visiting. And when there were visitors, she made it her business to know why they were visiting.

So when two strangers came to the city to Rahab's house – looking around and asking questions – she immediately knew who they were. They were spies from a nation of people called the Israelites.

She had heard about the Israelites: how their god, Yahweh, had dried up the waters of the Red Sea when

95

they came out of Egypt, and how they had completely destroyed Sihon and Og, two Amorite kings who had ruled east of the Jordan River. She had heard that Israel planned to invade and take over Jericho and that anyone who was not part of the tribes of Israel would be slaughtered and wiped off the face of the earth.

Rahab, like everyone else in Jericho, was terrified about what the Israelites planned to do. She also knew that the King of Jericho would be looking for the spies to stop them from going back with a report on the best way to capture the city of Jericho. Rahab weighed her options and decided that she would make a business deal with the spies.

When the King's messengers came looking for the spies, Rahab hid them. She told the messengers that she didn't know the men were spies. And she told them that the spies had already left the city, but if they hurried, they might be able to catch them.

Then Rahab went to the spies and propositioned them. She had saved their lives when the King's messengers came looking for them. In return, when the Israelites came to take over Jericho, she expected her life, along with the lives of her mother, father, sister, brother and all who belonged to her, to be spared.

This was the arrangement Rahab negotiated. This was the arrangement that the spies agreed to keep. And when the armies of Israel came to Jericho, before they destroyed the city, Rahab and all of her family were escorted outside of the city to safety.

Strength Affirmations

I can negotiate a better life for myself and the people I love. I will manage my business.

*****

Your Story—Your Strength

In what areas of your life have you
or will you affirm these strengths?

_____

_____

_____

_____

_____

_____

_____

_____

_____

_____

ACHSAH

Inspired by Joshua 15:13-19

*****

The Scripture

"And Caleb said, "Whoever attacks Kiriath-sepher and takes it, to him I will give my daughter Achsah as wife." Joshua 15:16

*****

Her Story

Achsah, like her father, was not shy about getting what she believed she had a right to have. Her father, Caleb, had taken possession of a large piece of land in Hebron. Before Caleb arrived, the land was controlled by three brothers. But Achsah's father, Caleb, was a warrior and was known to go after what he believed belonged to him. And so, in true warrior style, he ran the three brothers and their people out of the land of Hebron.

But that wasn't enough for him. He also wanted the land located in Debir, but he needed help getting it. So, he offered to give Achsah as a wife to the man who was able to capture and take away the land from the people of Debir. That man turned out to be Othniel. He captured Debir for Caleb, and Achsah became his wife. Achsah persuaded her husband to ask her father to give her part of the land he had taken in Hebron. Her father agreed and a piece of land in the dry, southern area of Hebron became hers.

But what was she supposed to do with this piece of land? She wouldn't be able to grow any food on it. The most it would be good for would be for cattle, sheep and goats to graze. And even though the land had enough grass for grazing, the animals couldn't live without water. And neither could Achsah and her family. Achsah refused to be shackled to land that couldn't produce food or sustain life. So, back to her father she went to ask for more.

As she made her way to her father, he saw that she had a sense of urgency about her. She didn't waste any time and she didn't mince any words, explaining to him that she needed more. She told him she was thankful for the land but it was in a dry area and nothing would grow. She told him she needed springs of water so that the land would produce and the animals wouldn't die of thirst.

Achsah was her father's daughter – determined, strong-willed, intelligent – very much like him and Caleb saw himself in her. And he knew she was right. The land by itself was not enough. She needed more. So, he gave her two springs of water, one in the upper region and one in the lower region of the land he had given her.

*****

Strength Affirmations

I am proactive. I can take initiative. I will ask for what
I need when what I have is not enough.

*****

Your Story—Your Strength

In what areas of your life have you
or will you affirm these strengths?

_____

_____

_____

_____

_____

_____

_____

_____

Kanisha L. Adkins

JAEL & DEBORAH

Inspired by Judges 4:17-24

*****

The Scripture

"Most blessed of women be Jael, the wife of Heber the Kenite, of tent-dwelling women most blessed."
Judges 5:24

*****

Her Story

No one would have ever suspected Jael. After all, she was just a woman and the wife of a Kenite. She wasn't an Israelite and she had no reason to be loyal to the people of Israel or their God. Perhaps her actions wouldn't be out of loyalty to them. Perhaps she would act to protect herself. Whatever her reasons may have been, when the Canaanite army captain Sisera ran into her tent, Jael had to think fast.

Jael didn't know if Sisera intended to rape her, kill her, or both. Men didn't enter women's tents for honorable reasons. And whatever his reason, Jael decided that she would fight for her life and for her honor. She welcomed him into her tent, or so he thought. He was exhausted, so she invited him to lie down, and she covered him with a blanket. He was thirsty, so she gave him milk to drink because she knew it would relax him. Within minutes, Sisera had fallen asleep.

Jael quietly picked up a hammer and a tent stake. Her heart was pounding and her hands were shaking.

She tiptoed over to where Sisera lay sleeping and, with every ounce of energy and strength that she had, she hammered the stake through the temple of his head and into the ground.

Minutes later, Jael heard several people talking outside of her tent. One of them was Barak, an Israelite soldier, asking some of the Kenite men if they had seen Sisera. Jael walked over to him and told him what she had done. Barak followed her into her tent and there on the floor lay Sisera – dead. Immediately, Barak remembered the words that Israel's prophet and judge Deborah had spoken to him. Barak had refused to follow God's command to pursue and kill Sisera. And because of Barak's disobedience, God had used a woman – Jael – to save Israel.

*****

Strength Affirmations

I am courageous, strategic and strong.
I have agency to overcome any problem.

*****

Your Story—Your Strength

In what areas of your life have you
or will you affirm these strengths?

_____

_____

_____

_____

_____

_____

_____

_____

DELILAH

Inspired by Judges 16:4-20

*****

The Scripture

"So Delilah said to Samson, "Please tell me what makes your strength so great, and how you could be bound, so that one could subdue you." Judges 16:6

*****

Her Story

Delilah was like no other woman Samson had ever met. She had an allure that challenged men, and it was no wonder that Samson fell in love with her. He had been instantly attracted when he first saw her. But the attraction didn't stop with her physical beauty. There was something about her mannerisms that drew Samson to her. It was the way she looked at him – the way she spoke to him – the way she touched him.

Samson was known as "Samson the strong man." He was a fighter. Single-handedly, he had killed a lion that came charging at him one day. On another day, in a fit of rage and without an army, he attacked 30 men and took all of their property. He was a wild, restless man. But there was something about Delilah that calmed him. Delilah gave him a place to rest, relax and lay his head. This was the Delilah that Samson loved. But in spite of his love for her, there was no indication that she loved him back. And in spite of the affection and tenderness she showed Samson, there was another side to Delilah – a side that was complex, calculating and self-serving.

107

This was the Delilah who was confronted by a group of Philistine leaders to make a deal with them: she would find out the secret to Samson's great strength (so that the Philistine's could tie him up and strip him of his strength) and they would each give her eleven hundred pieces of silver. It was the complex, calculating, self-serving Delilah who, day after day, asked Samson the secret to his strength and how he could be tied up and made weak.

It was the complex, calculating, self-serving Delilah who tied Samson up only to find out that he had lied to her and that he was able to break free with little to no effort. And it was the complex, calculating, self-serving Delilah who pressed and pushed until Samson finally told her that if his hair were ever to be shaved from his head, he would be like any other person.

Finally, Delilah knew that *this* was not a lie. She sent a message to the Philistine leaders telling them how to rob Samson of his strength. Delilah, herself, lulled Samson to sleep and had his head shaved. The Philistine leaders captured Samson, and Delilah was given her silver.

Years later, when people spoke about what had happened, they were always left wondering why she did it. No one understood why Delilah took the bribe. No one understood why she betrayed Samson. He loved her and, no doubt, would have provided for her and protected her for life. But this was obviously not good enough for her. She had found out Samson's truth and used it for her own personal gain, and for his harm. For that reason, not much good was ever spoken of her after that day – except for one thing. She was a woman who knew how to persist until she found out the truth.

Strength Affirmations

I am unshakable and determined.
I will persist until I find the truth.

*****

Your Story—Your Strength

In what areas of your life have you
or will you affirm these strengths?

_____

_____

_____

_____

_____

_____

_____

_____

_____

ORPAH, RUTH & NAOMI

Inspired by Ruth 1:1-14

*****

The Scripture

"Then they wept aloud again. Orpah kissed her mother-in-law, but Ruth clung to her." Ruth 1:14

*****

Her Story

It was time for Naomi to go back to Bethlehem– to her home, to her people. She had never intended to stay in Moab. And even though she looked forward to going home, her trip would be bittersweet because her husband and sons wouldn't be going with her.

Naomi's husband had died not long after they arrived in Moab. And her sons had died several years after their father. Still, Naomi had her daughters-in-law, and their presence brought her comfort and relief. But as the three women were headed to Bethlehem, Naomi thought: *it would be better for Ruth and Orpah to stay in Moab, their home.*

So, Naomi embraced and kissed Ruth and Orpah. She thanked them for the kindness and faithfulness they had shown to her and her sons. She prayed that God would bless each woman with another husband and another household. And she told them to go back.

Ruth and Orpah cried uncontrollably at Naomi's suggestion that they should go back. Their love for Naomi was deep, and they couldn't imagine life without her. Naomi cried too. She tried to push them away but they held her tighter. Frustrated and weary, she lashed out at them,

"Go back! Why are you clinging to me?! Go back! I don't have any more sons! I'm too old to get another husband. And even if I did, would you wait for me to have more sons? And would you wait for them to grow up?" (Ruth 1:11-13)

Orpah looked into her mother-in-law's eyes. She saw that the years in Moab had taken a toll on Naomi. She saw that the loss of her husband and sons had robbed Naomi of her joy. She thought about Naomi's words. As much as she wanted to go with her mother-in-law to Bethlehem, she knew that Naomi's words were filled with wisdom and experience.

Naomi's words were those of a woman who knew what it was like to live in Bethlehem *and* to live in Moab. They were the words of a woman who knew what it was like to live in an Israelite community *and* to live among the Moabite community. They were the words of a woman who knew what it was like to live with a people committed to one god, Yahweh, and to live with a people who believed in many gods.

Orpah wanted to go with Naomi because she loved her. But her admiration and her respect for Naomi were just as great as her love for Naomi. And so, out of respect for Naomi, *her elder,* Orpah went back – back to *her* mother's home, back to *her* people, *back to the life that was best for her.*

Strength Affirmations

I can choose the places that are appropriate for me.
I will decide where I belong.

*****

Your Story—Your Strength

In what areas of your life have you
or will you affirm these strengths?

_____

_____

_____

_____

_____

_____

_____

_____

Kanisha L. Adkins

HANNAH & PENINNAH

Inspired by 1 Samuel 1

*****

The Scripture

"But Hannah answered, "No, my lord, I am a woman deeply troubled; I have drunk neither wine nor strong drink, but I have been pouring out my soul before the LORD." 1 Samuel 1:15

*****

Her Story

Hannah had been married for several years, but she and her husband had not been able to have children. She knew how important it was to have children, particularly sons, to carry on the family name. She was sure that she would eventually become pregnant. So, she remained hopeful and didn't worry too much. That is, until her husband decided to take another wife.

The other wife, Peninnah, was quite fertile. Peninnah gave birth – to sons and daughters – almost every year during the first few years of marriage to Elkanah. Hannah felt more and more discouraged. She felt tormented by the birth of each of Peninnah's children. She couldn't understand why she hadn't been able to become pregnant. And she started to feel ostracized and pitied by her community. She saw the looks on the people's faces and she heard their whispers. *She was sure* they were talking about her – *condemning her for not giving her husband a son*. Her feelings of despair

115

were even worse when it came time for the yearly trip to the temple to worship and make sacrifices to God.

While they were at the temple, Elkanah divided the sacrifice into parts. He gave Peninnah and her children each a part of the sacrifice to offer to God. And even though Hannah didn't have a child, he gave her *two* parts to offer as a sacrifice, because he loved her and he could tell that she was upset about not having any children.

But the *double portion* to sacrifice wasn't enough. Hannah felt despised and ashamed. She wasn't able to eat or sleep. All she could do was cry. And no one seemed to understand or care about her disgrace: not her husband and definitely not Peninnah. So, Hannah turned to the only one whom she thought understood, cared and could take away her disgrace. She turned to God.

After the sacrifice, after everyone had finished eating, Hannah stayed in the temple, praying and crying hysterically, begging God to take away her shame by giving her a son. And she made a promise to God: if God would take away her shame – by giving her a son – she would give her son back to God, to serve in the temple, all the days of his life.

Hannah didn't think about how it would feel to give up her son. She just wanted the shame to be gone. That was the prayer and the promise that Hannah poured out of her heart. She went back to her home with Elkanah, and Peninnah and her children, believing that God had heard her and would answer her.

Eventually, Hannah became pregnant and had a son. She named him Samuel. She remembered her prayer – *that God would take away her shame* – and she knew that God had answered her prayer. But she also remembered her promise – *to give Samuel to God, to serve God in the temple with the priest*. Hannah would keep her promise. She would take Samuel to the temple as soon as he was on solid food. And as that day grew closer, Hannah felt just as much grief as she felt shame before she became pregnant. Samuel meant the world to her. But Hannah was as committed to the promise she had made as she had been committed to the prayer she had prayed. And when the time came, Hannah found the strength to give back to God the child that God had given to her.

*****

Strength Affirmations

I can give God those things that
mean the most to me. I can let go.

*****

Your Story—Your Strength

In what areas of your life have you
or will you affirm these strengths?

_____

_____

_____

_____

_____

_____

_____

_____

_____

AFTERWORD

I wrote this book to introduce you to some women who may not be familiar to you. I also wrote this book to present to you a more positive side of some women who you *have* heard of but whose stories have often been negative or secondary to a male, main character.

No longer should we gloss over these women as flat and one dimensional, or confine them to the role of being dependent and pitiful characters. No longer should we rush past, or stumble over their names in biblical texts in order to get to more familiar names and stories.

My hope is that we will give these women a chance – when we read and hear their stories in our worship services, in our bible studies, in our private devotionals, and in our search for knowledge and enlightenment. Give these women a chance.

Give them a chance to be fully human and to be fully engaged in *their* lives. Talk about them in your women's groups. Teach your daughters and granddaughters about them. Introduce them to your nieces and the young ladies whom you mentor. And please – tell the men in your life about them.

Say their names. Learn their stories. And give their stories a chance – the stories in the biblical texts and those stories created by my *sanctified imagination*. Find inspiration in the stories of who they were and in the stories of who they might have been. Look to them as models of strength in the ordinary and in the extraordinary areas of your life.

My hope is that you will sit with these women in the days ahead. Acknowledge their challenges and what are considered as weaknesses. But don't abandon or reject them as meaningless or dispensable. Redeem them from the stories that have dismissed them. Reflect on the struggles that have shaped them. And appropriate their strengths as your own.

There are at least 111 *named* women in the Old Testament. This is just the beginning. There's more to come.

Made in the USA
Columbia, SC
23 December 2018